URUGUAY 2016 HUMAN RIGHTS REPORT

EXECUTIVE SUMMARY

The Oriental Republic of Uruguay is a constitutional republic with an elected president and a bicameral legislature. In 2014, in a free and fair runoff election, Tabare Vazquez won a five-year presidential term, and his Frente Amplio party won a majority in parliament.

Civilian authorities maintained effective control over the security forces.

Principal human rights problems included widespread use of extended pretrial detention, severe overcrowding and harsh conditions in some prisons, and violence against women.

Other human rights concerns included violence against children, societal discrimination against Afro-Uruguayans, and trafficking in persons.

The government took steps to prosecute officials who committed abuses, and there were no reports of impunity during the year.

Section 1. Respect for the Integrity of the Person, Including Freedom from:

a. Arbitrary Deprivation of Life and other Unlawful or Politically Motivated Killings

There were no reports that the government or its agents committed arbitrary or unlawful killings.

b. Disappearance

There were no reports of politically motivated disappearances.

c. Torture and Other Cruel, Inhuman, or Degrading Treatment or Punishment

The constitution and law prohibit such practices, and there were no reports that government officials employed them.

In August 2015 a judge indicted 26 employees of the Uruguayan Institute for Children and Adolescents (INAU) Adolescent Offenders' Division (SIRPA) for abuses of juveniles at the Ceprili home for youth. In June an internal INAU investigation determined the employees did not torture the juveniles, and in December an appeals court acquitted 14 of the 26 employees. The crime, initially classified as "torture," was changed to "abuse of authority" for the remaining 12 employees.

Prison and Detention Center Conditions

Prison and detention center conditions continued to be harsh and potentially life threatening in some facilities.

Physical Conditions: The National Rehabilitation Institute (INR) reported 10,228 prisoners in facilities with a capacity for approximately 9,095 inmates. Approximately 65 percent of the prisoners were awaiting sentencing. Some facilities had inadequate sanitation, heating, ventilation, lighting, medical care, and access to potable water. Prisoners depended on visitors for clothing and lacked sufficient food to reach their daily minimum caloric intake. Female and poorer male prisoners often received no support from their families.

Some prison facilities were inadequate. Many lacked formal clearances from the fire department. The INR closed the El Molino facility in Montevideo due to poor building conditions and transferred nine women with 10 accompanying children to an annex of the Unidad Penitenciaria No.5. The public mental health hospitals Vilardebo, Colonia Etchepare, and Santin Carlos Rossi, which held prisoners, suffered overcrowding and infrastructure problems.

In April and June, Juan Miguel Petit, the country's special rapporteur on the prison system, reported that the conditions of modules 8, 10, and 11 of unit 4 of Comcar prison were very bad. The report described inadequate building conditions, rodent infestation, poor hygiene of inmates, overcrowding, and insufficient space designated for work, educational activities, and family visits. The report also stated few inmates had access to exercise activities and noted a lack of reliable medical attention, due to understaffing. The rapporteur alerted prison authorities to a serious problem of internal violence in several prison facilities and requested urgent action.

Five prisoners died in these facilities in the first half of the year due to violence. In September a male prisoner died in one of the units of Comcar prison as the result of prisoner-on-prisoner violence. In an overcrowded facility in the department of Maldonado, prisoners set fire to mattresses and caused damage to the prison infrastructure. Two police officers were injured during the incident. Lawyers provided to prisoners who could not afford legal counseling held video conferences with their clients due to unsafe conditions that prevented them from visiting modules 8, 10, and 11.

In December 2015 the government created INISA to replace SIRPA, and in June INISA authorities took over management of the organization. According to the new director, many facilities were aging or damaged and could not be refurbished due to budget limitations, which additionally affected hiring staff. An audit of the buildings presented by the Bureau of Architecture in the Ministry of Transportation and Public Works concluded that most facilities were inadequate to develop and implement rehabilitation programs.

In July the Pan American Health Organization presented the results of a 2015 poll on prisoner health conditions. The report noted that four of 10 prisoners were overweight or obese due to lack of physical activity, medical treatment was inadequate, and 74 percent of prisoners smoked tobacco and 33 percent smoked marijuana. In addition, 19 percent took psychotropic drugs without prescriptions or medical controls, 5 percent consumed cocaine paste, and 3 percent consumed cocaine powder. Slightly more than 8 percent attempted suicide, and 18 percent alleged suffering mistreatment.

In August the government's National Mechanism for the Prevention of Torture reported as major problems the lack of sufficiently trained staff, poor building conditions that resulted in overcrowding and violence, and insufficient social and educational activities. Concerning INISA facilities, the report noted pervasive use of psychotropic drugs, with scarce medical control.

In September the labor union for law enforcement personnel expressed concern over the working conditions of police officers and civilian prison staff members in some facilities. Union representatives noted unhealthy and dangerous labor conditions, such as extended work hours (shifts of 12 to 18 hours) and unmanageable responsibilities, including an instance where a single guard, without adequate communication systems, was in charge of monitoring 700 detainees.

Administration: Independent authorities investigated allegations of inhuman conditions. The Office of Probation Measures continued to lack sufficient human and financial resources to work in most departments.

<u>Independent Monitoring</u>: The government permitted monitoring by independent nongovernmental observers, local human rights groups, media, the International Committee of the Red Cross, and international bodies. The country's special rapporteur on the prison system and the National Institution of Human Rights (INDDHH) were also allowed to monitor prisons.

<u>Improvements</u>: In March the State Health Services Administration collaborated with the INR on a program to provide medical and psychological support to drug-addicted prisoners in Montevideo. In May officials from the INR and INISA participated in six workshops on prison management led by experts from a foreign country.

Authorities provided inmates several new options for work, both during incarceration and after release. The government's budget law created the National Unit to Support Released Prisoners. The INR and the National Institute for Employment and Professional Training signed an agreement to teach prisoners skills in garment making, construction, carpentry, cooking, and vegetable gardening. In February volunteer prisoners joined municipal workers of the department of Salto to clean up the city after major floods. The Salto municipality also agreed to hire 16 inmates, who were allowed to leave the prison compound on a regular basis to do work for the community. In September the Ministry of Interior and the Canelones municipality signed an agreement for 27 prisoners to repair sidewalks and lanes at a local resort. In June a private fishing-port services operator in Montevideo began hiring former prisoners for its operations. The INR created industrial sites in the departments of Canelones, Maldonado, and Salto to help prisoner rehabilitation.

Government authorities and private entities also provided other opportunities for adult prisoners to participate in sports activities, such as soccer and rugby. In June INISA began a pilot program to train juvenile inmates in sports to allow them to compete in events at the national level.

d. Arbitrary Arrest or Detention

The law and constitution prohibit arbitrary arrest and detention, and the government generally observed these prohibitions.

Role of the Police and Security Apparatus

The National Police, under the Ministry of Interior, maintain internal security. The National Directorate for Migration, also under the Ministry of Interior, is responsible for migration and border enforcement. Civilian authorities maintained effective control over the National Police, and the government has effective mechanisms to investigate and punish abuse and corruption. The armed forces, under the Ministry of National Defense, are responsible for external security and have some domestic responsibilities as guardians of the outside perimeter of six prisons. There were no reports of impunity involving police and security forces during the year.

The judiciary continued to investigate the serious human rights violations committed during the 1973-1985 military dictatorship. The law classifies crimes committed during the dictatorship as crimes against humanity. The nongovernmental organization (NGO) Truth and Justice Group was responsible for further investigating human rights abuses committed between 1968 and 1985.

Arrest Procedures and Treatment of Detainees

Police apprehended suspects with warrants issued by a duly authorized official and brought them before an independent judiciary. The law provides detainees with the right to a prompt judicial determination of the legality of detention and requires that the detaining authority explain the legal grounds for the detention. For any detainee who cannot afford a defense attorney, the court appoints a public defender at no cost to the detainee. The constitution states police cannot hold persons for longer than 24 hours without informing a judge. The judge then has another 24 hours to determine whether the subjects will be indicted and detained, indicted but released on their own recognizance, or released for lack of probable cause. If no charges are brought, the case is filed but the investigation may continue and the case reopened if new evidence emerges.

The possibility of bail exists but was not used in practice. For most persons accused of crimes punishable by at least two years in prison, the criminal code procedure prohibits bail. A judge may set bail if the individual is a first-time offender and if there are provisions in place to prevent the subject from fleeing. Most persons facing lesser charges were not jailed. Officials allowed detainees prompt access to family members.

Confessions obtained by police prior to a detainee's appearance before a judge and without an attorney present are not valid. A lawyer assigned to each police station reports to the Ministry of Interior concerning treatment of detainees. A judge leads the investigation of a detainee's claim of mistreatment.

<u>Pretrial Detention</u>: The use of pretrial detention is mandatory for particular crimes, and lengthy legal procedures required in the judge-led, inquisitorial criminal justice system, large numbers of detainees, and staff shortages in the judicial system led to trial delays and prison overcrowding. Some detainees spent one year or more in jail awaiting the conclusion of their trial. For most individuals credibly accused of crimes punishable by at least two years' incarceration, the accused is sent to prison pending trial. First-time offenders (with no criminal record) and individuals facing lesser charges are usually released pending trial. The number of instances in which the length of pretrial detention equaled or exceeded the maximum sentence for the alleged crime could not be determined due to a lack of statistics.

<u>Detainee's Ability to Challenge Lawfulness of Detention before a Court</u>: Persons are entitled to challenge in court the legal basis or arbitrary nature of their detention and obtain prompt release and compensation if found to have been unlawfully detained.

e. Denial of Fair Public Trial

The constitution provides for an independent judiciary, and the other branches of government generally respected judicial independence.

Trial Procedures

The constitution provides for the right to a fair trial, and an independent judiciary generally enforced this right. Defendants have the right to a presumption of innocence, to be informed promptly and in detail of the charges brought against them, to have a trial without undue delay, to be present at their trial, to communicate with an attorney of their choice (or have one provided at public expense if unable to pay), to have adequate time and facilities to prepare a defense, to receive free interpretation as necessary from the moment charged through all appeals, to access government-held evidence, to not be compelled to testify or confess guilt, and to appeal. Defendants may cross-examine witnesses against them and present witnesses and evidence on their own behalf. The law extends these rights to all citizens.

Juries are not used; trial proceedings usually consist of written arguments to the judge and were not normally made public. Only the judge, prosecutor, and defense attorney have access to the written record. Individual judges may elect to hear oral arguments, but most judges chose to rule on a case solely based on an examination of written documents, a major factor slowing down the judicial process.

Political Prisoners and Detainees

There were no reports of political prisoners or detainees.

Civil Judicial Procedures and Remedies

There are transparent administrative procedures to handle complaints of abuse by government agents. An independent and impartial judiciary handles civil disputes, but its decisions were ineffectively enforced. Local police lacked the training and staff to enforce restraining orders, which often were generated during civil disputes related to domestic violence. Cases involving violations of an individual's human rights may be submitted through petitions filed by individuals or organizations to the Inter-American Commission of Human Rights, which in turn may submit the case to the Inter-American Court of Human Rights. The court may order civil remedies including fair compensation to the individual injured.

f. Arbitrary or Unlawful Interference with Privacy, Family, Home, or Correspondence

The law prohibits such actions, and there were no reports that the government failed to respect these prohibitions.

Section 2. Respect for Civil Liberties, Including:

a. Freedom of Speech and Press

The law provides for freedom of speech and press, and the government generally respected these rights. An independent press, an effective judiciary, and a functioning democratic political system combined to promote freedom of speech and press.

Internet Freedom

The government did not restrict or disrupt access to the internet or censor online content, and there were no credible reports that the government monitored private online communications without appropriate legal authority.

According to the International Telecommunication Union, 65 percent of the population used the internet in 2015.

Academic Freedom and Cultural Events

There were no government restrictions on academic freedom or cultural events.

b. Freedom of Peaceful Assembly and Association

The law provides for the freedoms of assembly and association, and the government generally respected these rights.

c. Freedom of Religion

See the Department of State's *International Religious Freedom Report* at www.state.gov/religiousfreedomreport/.

d. Freedom of Movement, Internally Displaced Persons, Protection of Refugees, and Stateless Persons

The law provides for freedom of internal movement, foreign travel, emigration, and repatriation, and the government generally respected these rights. The government cooperated with the Office of the UN High Commissioner for Refugees and other humanitarian organizations in providing protection and assistance to internally displaced persons, refugees, returning refugees, asylum seekers, stateless persons, and other persons of concern.

Protection of Refugees

Access to Asylum: The law provides for the granting of asylum or refugee status, and the government has established a system for providing protection to refugees. Through its refugee commission, the government had a system for adjudicating asylum claims, providing protection to refugees, and finding durable solutions, including resettlement.

Durable Solutions: There were approximately 350-370 refugees in the country, mostly from Latin America, who received long-term support. The government continued to provide 42 Syrian refugees with temporary housing, financial assistance, food, clothing, language training, and employment training.

Section 3. Freedom to Participate in the Political Process

The law provides citizens the ability to choose their government in free and fair periodic elections held by secret ballot and based on universal and equal suffrage.

Elections and Political Participation

Recent Elections: In 2014 Tabare Vazquez of the Frente Amplio (Broad Front) party won a five-year presidential term in a free and fair runoff election. The runoff followed a series of party primaries and a free and fair first-round election involving seven political parties. In parliamentary elections in October 2015, the Frente Amplio won 15 of 30 seats in the Chamber of Senators and 50 of 99 seats in the Chamber of Representatives.

Participation of Women and Minorities: No laws limit the participation of women and members of minorities in the political process. Women participated in the political process and government, although primarily at lower and middle levels. Afro-Uruguayans were underrepresented in government; there were two Afro-Uruguayans among the 99 representatives in parliament.

Section 4. Corruption and Lack of Transparency in Government

The law provides criminal penalties for corruption by officials, and the government generally implemented the law effectively. While officials sometimes engaged in corrupt practices that authorities addressed with appropriate legal action, the country was considered to have a low level of corruption, according to Transparency International.

Corruption: No cases of official corruption occurred or were publicized during the year.

Financial Disclosure: The law requires income and asset disclosure by appointed and elected officials. Each year the presidentially appointed Transparency and Ethics Board lists the names of government officials expected to file a declaration on its web page and informs the individuals' organizations of those expected to comply. The incumbent, the judiciary, a special parliamentary committee, or the board may access the information in the declarations (by majority vote of the board). The board may direct an official's office to retain 50 percent of the employee's salary until the declaration is presented, and it may publish the names of those who fail to comply in the federal register. While there is a requirement for filing, there is no review of the filings absent an allegation of wrongdoing.

Public Access to Information: The law provides for general access to public information, defined as all information held by a government entity unless considered classified. The law requires government agencies to make public their organizational charts, responsibilities, salaries, and budget allotment and to produce regular reports. Authorities effectively implemented the law; there were no public outreach activities to encourage its use.

Section 5. Governmental Attitude Regarding International and Nongovernmental Investigation of Alleged Violations of Human Rights

A number of domestic and international human rights groups generally operated without government restriction, investigating and publishing their findings on human rights cases. Government officials often were cooperative and responsive to their views.

Government Human Rights Bodies: The INDDHH, an autonomous agency that reports to parliament, is composed of five board members proposed by civil society organizations and approved by a two-thirds vote in parliament's General Assembly for a period of five years (renewable one time). According to the most recently available information, the institution received 152 complaints and 416 requests for guidance in 2015, primarily concerning personal integrity, access to jobs, equality and nondiscrimination, and access to justice.

The institution worked with the prison ombudsman, who reported to parliament. It did not deal with human rights violations committed during the military dictatorship (1973-1985), which were handled by the Human Rights Secretariat in the Office of the Presidency.

The Committee against Racism, Xenophobia, and All Forms of Discrimination of the Ministry of Education and Culture includes government, religious, and civil society representatives. The committee had not been allocated a budget since 2010 but received economic support from the government for some activities. Government agency representatives on the commission received no extra compensation but were able to participate in the commission's activities during work hours. Members of civil society participated on an ad hoc basis without any additional compensation.

Section 6. Discrimination, Societal Abuses, and Trafficking in Persons

Women

Rape and Domestic Violence: The law criminalizes rape, including spousal rape. The law allows for sentences of two to 12 years' imprisonment for a person found guilty of rape, and authorities effectively enforced the law. The Ministry of Interior attributed 62 percent (29 cases) of homicides to domestic violence in the 12-month period ending October 31. Tacuarembo, Treinta y Tres, and Rocha Departments had the highest incidence of femicide.

The law criminalizes domestic violence, including physical, psychological, and sexual violence, but victims without severe injuries often did not file complaints. Victims of domestic violence requiring hospitalization were more likely to receive follow-up assistance from health-care providers and police authorities.

The law allows for sentences of six months' to two years' imprisonment for a person found guilty of committing an act of violence or making continued threats of violence. Civil courts decided most of the domestic cases, and judges in these cases often issued restraining orders, which were difficult to enforce. The judiciary and the Ministry of Interior continued the use of double ankle-bracelet sets (one bracelet for the victim and one for the aggressor) to track the distance between the perpetrator and victim. During the year there were 346 sets of ankle bracelets in use, compared with 283 in 2015.

The Ministry of Social Development, some police stations in the interior, INAU, and NGOs operated shelters where abused women and children could seek temporary refuge. In 2015, 58 women and 99 children received temporary refuge in these shelters. All services were funded and staffed according to the reported prevalence of domestic violence in each location; nonetheless, NGOs and government actors reported the shelters were often overcrowded. The Montevideo municipal government and the state-owned telephone company Antel funded a free nationwide hotline operated by trained NGO employees for victims of domestic violence.

The government's 2016-2019 Action Plan For a Life Free of Gender-Based Violence provided interagency coordination on violence prevention, access to justice, victim protection and attention, and punishment of perpetrators. It also promoted social and cultural awareness and provided training for public servants to deal more effectively with gender-based violence. The Prosecutor General's

Office established a specialized gender unit in September to incorporate a gender perspective in the agency's work, promote greater respect for women's rights, combat gender-based violence, and enhance interagency coordination on gender issues.

The National Institute of Women and the National Institute of Employment and Professional Training signed an agreement to offer job skills training to female victims of domestic violence and discrimination.

Sexual Harassment: The law prohibits sexual harassment in the workplace and punishes it by fines or dismissal. The law establishes guidelines for the prevention of sexual harassment in the workplace, as well as in student-professor relations, and provides damages for survivors.

Reproductive Rights: Couples and individuals have the right to decide the number, spacing, and timing of their children; manage their reproductive health; and have access to the information and means to do so, free from discrimination, coercion, or violence.

Discrimination: The law grants the same legal status and rights for women as for men. Women, however, faced discrimination in employment, pay, credit, education, housing, and business ownership. The law does not require equal pay for equal work. In May, UN Women Deputy Regional Representative Lara Blanco noted that women's access to jobs increased by 3 percent in 2015 but that a 20 percent difference remained, compared with men's access to jobs.

Children

Birth Registration: Citizenship is derived by birth within the country's territory and/or from one's parents. The government immediately registered all births.

Child Abuse: The System for the Protection of Childhood and Adolescence Against Violence (SIPIAV) reported 44 cases of child abuse in 2015, mostly corresponding to sexual and psychological abuse. INAU reported 1,908 cases of violence against children in 2015. INAU's hotline reported receiving 8,720 calls for information and requests for assistance in 2015, the latest period for which information was available. A UN Children's Fund (UNICEF) report published in June noted that despite improvements, 54 percent of children under age 14 were victims of some kind of "violent discipline" at home--more so in urban areas than in rural ones. Thirty-four percent of boys and 18 percent of girls suffered physical and psychological aggressions.

The government sponsored awareness campaigns against child abuse. SIPIAV-- which was led by INAU and included representatives from the Ministries of Social Development, of Health, and of Interior; the judicial branch; UNICEF; NGOs; and the National Education Board--coordinated interagency efforts regarding protection of children's rights.

Early and Forced Marriage: The legal minimum age for marriage is 18, but with parental consent it is 12 for girls and 14 for boys. Early marriage was not perceived to be a significant problem.

Sexual Exploitation of Children: The law prohibits the commercial sexual exploitation of children and child pornography, and authorities made efforts to enforce the law through investigations and prosecutions. The law does not specifically criminalize prostitution of children as child sex trafficking. The penal code establishes the minimum age for consensual sex as 12. When a sexual union takes place between an adult and a minor under age 15, violence is presumed and statutory rape laws, which carry a penalty of two to 12 years in prison, may be applied. Minors between ages 12 and 15 may legally engage in consensual sex with each other. Penalties for trafficking children range from four to 16 years in prison. Child pornography is illegal, and penalties range from one to six years in prison. Some children were victims of commercial sexual exploitation, pornography, and sex trafficking. Laws against child pornography were effectively enforced.

In December the Ministry of Social Development presented a report of the National Committee for the Eradication of Commercial and Noncommercial Sexual Exploitation of Children on sexual exploitation of children and adolescents. The report noted the committee assisted with 285 cases during the year.

Institutionalized Children: INAU's 2015 annual report stated 511 adolescents were in INISA homes (see section 1.c., Prison and Detention Center Conditions).

International Child Abductions: The country is a party to the 1980 Hague Convention on the Civil Aspects of International Child Abduction. See the Department of State's *Annual Report on International Parental Child Abduction* at travel.state.gov/content/childabduction/en/legal/compliance.html.

Anti-Semitism

The Jewish Central Committee reported that the Jewish community had an estimated population of 15,000.

In March businessman and community leader David Fremd was stabbed to death in the city of Paysandu by a schoolteacher allegedly aligned with anti-Jewish movements. Police arrested Carlos Omar Peralta, and a judge indicted him for the murder of Fremd and religious hatred and requested a psychiatric evaluation. The psychiatric report stated Peralta's mental condition could not make him legally responsible for the crime. He was committed to Vilardebo, a public mental-health hospital.

In January the government granted media networks time to broadcast a commemorative message for International Holocaust Day. In May the government's Plan Ceibal program (digital connectivity for education) presented a project on the memory and legacy of the Holocaust. In November, President Tabare Vazquez participated in B'nai B'rith Uruguay's annual commemoration of Kristallnacht.

The Canelones municipality in the department of Canelones accepted a petition from the Jewish community to modify local cemetery regulations that require a minimum of 12 hours post mortem for burials.

Trafficking in Persons

See the Department of State's *Trafficking in Persons Report* at www.state.gov/j/tip/rls/tiprpt/.

Persons with Disabilities

The law prohibits discrimination against persons with physical, sensory, intellectual, and mental disabilities in employment, education, air travel and other transportation, access to health care, or the provision of other state services. The law prohibits abuse of persons with disabilities in educational and mental facilities, including degrading treatment, arbitrary commitment, and abusive use of physical restraints; unhygienic conditions; inadequate or dangerous medical care; and sexual or other violence. The law also grants persons with disabilities the right to vote and participate in civic affairs without restriction. The government in general did not monitor compliance and did not effectively enforce provisions or promote programs to provide for access to buildings, information, public transportation, and communications.

PRONADIS is the governmental entity responsible for developing actions, programs, and regulations to provide building and facilities access; cultural, sports and recreational opportunities; education; and employment to persons with disabilities. The Ministry of Social Development continued to train government employees on the content of the manual of good practices in dealing with persons with disabilities and to organize training workshops for government employees. In September the Ministry of Tourism and Ministry of Social Development signed an agreement to raise awareness, strengthen social inclusion, and improve access to travel opportunities for persons with disabilities. The Ministry of Tourism held an award ceremony to honor companies committed to good practices in providing access for persons with disabilities.

The law reserves no less than 4 percent of public-sector jobs for persons with physical and mental disabilities. Government decrees certify and regulate the use of canes and establish provisions for extending adequate training in their use. Guide dogs legally have full access to public and private premises and transportation. Most public buses did not have provisions for passengers with disabilities other than one reserved seat, although airports and ports offered accessibility accommodations. The law also provides tax benefits to private-sector companies and grants priority benefits to small and medium-sized companies owned by persons with disabilities.

The law grants children with disabilities the right to attend school (primary, secondary, and higher education). Ramps built at public elementary and high schools facilitated access for wheelchair users, and 87 percent of children and adolescents with disabilities attended school, including institutions of higher education. The state-funded University of the Republic offered sign-language interpreters for deaf students. Some movie theaters and other cultural venues lacked access ramps. Plan Ceibal continued to offer specially adapted laptops to children with disabilities. Some parks in Montevideo and Canelones offered wheelchair-accessible facilities.

National/Racial/Ethnic Minorities

The country's Afro-Uruguayan minority, estimated at 8 percent of the population, continued to face societal discrimination and high levels of poverty. Twenty-six percent of the Ministry of Social Development welfare program (Tarjeta Uruguay

Social) was directed to members of the Afro-Uruguayan community. The law grants 8 percent of state jobs to Afro-Uruguayan minority candidates who comply with constitutional and legal requirements. In 2015 Afro-Uruguayans held only 2.7 percent of state jobs. The National Employment Agency is required to include Afro-Uruguayans in its training courses. The law also requires that all scholarship and student support programs include a quota for Afro-Uruguayans, and it grants financial benefits to companies that hire them. An interagency antidiscrimination committee and the National Institution of Human Rights receive complaints of racism.

NGOs reported "structural racism" in society and noted that the percentage of Afro-Uruguayans working as unskilled laborers was much higher than for other groups. Afro-Uruguayans were underrepresented in government (two representatives in parliament and the president of the National Postal Service were Afro-Uruguayan), academia, and in the middle and upper echelons of private-sector firms. Unemployment of Afro-Uruguayan women remained high. The NGO Mundo Afro continued its AM radio talk show to raise awareness of racism and its antidiscrimination campaign through a network of informal AM radio stations; other outreach efforts included regional exhibitions and seminars for government employees responsible for staff recruitment.

As head of the government's ethnic and racial equality efforts, the Ministry of Social Development declared July the first Month of Afro-descendants. In July the ministry and the African Descent and Public Policies Department of the University of the Republic organized a seminar on Afro-descendant issues. The ministry organized a workshop on public policies about combatting structural racism.

In August the National Public Education Administration and Ministry of Social Development presented the guide *Education and Afro-descent* for teachers to use in their classrooms. The guide included modules that stress the use of the term Afro-descendant over other terms, recommended that teachers cite prominent Afro-Uruguayan leaders of the community in teaching the country's history, emphasized diversity as a positive value, and provided interactive tools with displays of African cultural activities that could be complemented with Afro-Uruguayan cultural education. In September the President's Office of Planning and Budget and the School of Humanities and Educational Sciences at the University of the Republic signed an agreement to carry out a study on the impact of racism and discrimination on the Afro-Uruguayan community.

The National Police Academy, National School for Peacekeeping Operations of Uruguay, and Ministry of Foreign Affairs' School of Diplomacy included discrimination awareness training as part of their curricula. Mundo Afro's Higher Institute for Afro Training offered courses related to Afro-descendant culture. In 2015 the Ministry of Interior created an Ethnic and Racial Affairs Unit.

Acts of Violence, Discrimination, and Other Abuses Based on Sexual Orientation and Gender Identity

The law prohibits discrimination based on sexual orientation and gender identity. Authorities generally protected the rights of lesbian, gay, bisexual, transgender, and intersex (LGBTI) persons, although civil society representatives asserted that generally government mechanisms for protection were weak and ineffective. Public-health regulations prevent gay men who had same-sex intercourse within 12 months to donate blood.

Members of the transgender community claimed to suffer social discrimination in society and within their families.

In June the Ministry of Public Health released a sexual diversity guide for professionals in the health sector and for the general public. The guide was cosponsored by the Medical School of the University of the Republic, the NGO Ovejas Negras, and the UN Population Fund.

In December 2015 the Montevideo municipality created a Diversity Secretariat and elaborated a plan of action for 2016-2020. The LGBT Chamber of Commerce, created in 2015, continued to expand agreements with departmental governments to foster diversity tourism programs.

HIV and AIDS Social Stigma

There were isolated reports of societal discrimination against persons with HIV/AIDS. In June public health authorities presented a 2015 report stating only 70-75 percent of individuals infected with HIV were diagnosed and that the infection had increased in men ages 15-24.

Section 7. Worker Rights

a. Freedom of Association and the Right to Collective Bargaining

The law, including related regulations and statutory instruments, protects the right of workers to form and join independent unions, conduct legal strikes, and bargain collectively, and the government respected and effectively enforced these rights in practice. The government and employers respected freedom of association and the right to collective bargaining in practice. Civil servants, employees of state-run enterprises, private-enterprise workers, and legal foreign workers may join unions. The law regulates collective bargaining and grants the government a significant role in adjudicating labor disputes. The law also designates trade unions to negotiate on behalf of workers whose companies are not unionized. The law prohibits antiunion discrimination and requires employers to reinstate workers fired for union activities and pay an indemnity to such workers. In addition, if an employer contracts employees from a third-party firm, the law holds the employer responsible for possible labor infringements committed by the third-party firm. Both foreign and domestic workers in the informal sector were excluded from these protections. The International Labor Organization urged the government to ensure that women caregivers for abandoned children have the right to form or join a trade union and bargain collectively.

The Collective Bargaining Division of the Ministry of Labor and Social Security investigates antiunion discrimination claims filed by union members. Information on government remedies and penalties for violations were not provided. There were generally effective, albeit lengthy, mechanisms for resolving workers' complaints against employers. The law establishes a conciliatory process before a trial begins and requires that the employer be informed of the reason for a claim and the alleged amount owed to the worker.

Worker organizations operated free of government and political intervention. The governing Frente Amplio party provided strong political support to labor unions in general, and they were very active in the political and economic life of the country. Collective bargaining occurred regularly. Workers exercised the right to strike.

b. Prohibition of Forced or Compulsory Labor

The law prohibits all forms of forced or compulsory labor, and the government effectively enforced applicable laws. The law establishes penalties of two to 12 years of prison for forced labor. Penalties were sufficient to deter violations. The labor ministry and other authorities did not report identifying or investigating cases of forced labor during the year. Information on the effectiveness of inspections and governmental remedies was not available. Foreign workers remained vulnerable to forced labor in agriculture and domestic service.

Also see the Department of State's *Trafficking in Persons Report* at
www.state.gov/j/tip/rls/tiprpt/.

c. Prohibition of Child Labor and Minimum Age for Employment

The law sets the minimum age for employment at age 15, but INAU may issue
work permits for children ages 13 to 15 under special circumstances specified by
law. Minors ages 15 to 18 must have government permission to work, undergo
physical exams prior to beginning work, and renew the exams yearly to confirm
the work being performed does not exceed the physical capacity of the incumbent.
The government maintains a list of hazardous or fatiguing work that minors should
not perform and for which it does not grant permits. Children ages 15 to 18 may
not work more than six hours per day within a 36-hour workweek and may not
work between 10 p.m. and 6 a.m.

The labor ministry is responsible for overall compliance with labor regulations, but
INAU is responsible for enforcing child labor laws. Violations of child labor laws
by companies and individuals are punishable by fines determined by an adjustable
government index. Parents of minors may receive a sentence of three months to
four years in prison, according to the penal code. These penalties were sufficient
to deter violations.

Due to a lack of dedicated resources, enforcement was mixed and particularly poor
in the informal economy, where most child labor occurred.

In 2015, the latest year for which data was available, INAU granted 3,132 work
permits. The main labor activities deemed nonhazardous were in the food industry
(supermarkets, fast food restaurants, and bakeries) and on small farms and poultry
farms; typical activities included clerical work, egg sorting, animal feeding, and
cleaning. In 2015, the latest year for which data was available, INAU worked with
the labor ministry and the National Insurance Bank to investigate 48 complaints of
child labor and worked with the Ministry of Interior to allow the judiciary to
prosecute cases. INAU had 11 trained child-labor inspectors, who completed
3,032 inspections in 2015. INAU continued its efforts to prevent and regulate
child labor and provided training on child labor matters.

Child labor continued to be reported in activities such as domestic service, street
vending, garbage collection and recycling, construction in the informal sector, and
in agriculture and forestry sectors, which were generally less strictly regulated and

where children often worked with their families. The most recent data available from the National Committee for the Eradication of Child Labor indicated that approximately 67,000 children and adolescents worked. A small percentage of children ages five to 17 begged for a living. Children were also exploited in commercial sexual exploitation (see section 6, Children).

Also see the Department of Labor's *Findings on the Worst Forms of Child Labor* at www.dol.gov/ilab/reports/child-labor/findings/.

d. Discrimination with Respect to Employment and Occupation

Labor laws and regulations prohibit discrimination with respect to employment and occupation on the basis of race, color, sex, religion, political opinion, national origin or citizenship, social origin, disability, sexual orientation and/or gender identity, age, language, HIV-positive status, or other communicable diseases. The government in general effectively enforced applicable law and regulations.

Discrimination in employment and occupation occurred with respect to sex and race. The government took steps to prevent and eliminate discrimination (see sections 5 and 6).

e. Acceptable Conditions of Work

The monthly minimum wage for all workers was 11,150 pesos ($395). The official per capita poverty income level was approximately 10,740 pesos ($380) per month, according to the National Statistics Institute.

The law stipulates that the standard workweek for those in the industrial and retail sectors may not exceed 44 or 48 hours with daily breaks of 30 minutes to two and one-half hours, depending on the sector. The law requires that workers receive premium pay for work in excess of regular work schedule hours. The law entitles all workers to 20 days of paid vacation after one year of employment and to paid annual holidays, and it prohibits compulsory overtime beyond a maximum 50-hour workweek. Employers in the industrial sector are required to give workers either Sunday off or one day off every six days of work (variable workweek). Workers in the retail sector are entitled to a 36-hour block of free time each week.

The labor ministry sets occupational safety and health standards, and the standards are current and appropriate for the main industries in the country. The law and regulations protect the rights of foreign and national workers in the formal sector but does not extend protection to the informal economy or female foster caregivers for abandoned children who provide services on behalf of INAU.

Except in the informal sector, workers, including domestic and migrant workers and workers in the agricultural sector, are covered by laws on minimum wage, hours of work, and occupational health and safety standards. Agricultural workers had a slightly higher minimum wage.

The labor ministry is responsible for enforcing the minimum monthly wage for both public- and private-sector employees and for enforcing legislation regulating health and safety conditions. The ministry had 120 labor inspectors. The number of penalties imposed for labor violations was unavailable, and penalties appeared to be insufficient to deter violations of labor laws in all cases. The ministry conducted 17,102 inspections in 2015.

The government monitored wages and other benefits, such as social security and health insurance, through the Social Security Fund and the Internal Revenue Service. The Ministry of Public Health's Bureau of Environment and Occupational Work is responsible for developing policies to detect, analyze, prevent, and control risk factors that may affect workers' health. In general authorities effectively enforced these standards in the formal sector but less so in the informal sector.

The labor ministry's Social Security Fund monitored domestic work and may obtain judicial authorization to conduct home inspections to investigate potential labor law violations. The law establishes August 19 as a paid holiday to recognize the Day of Domestic Workers. The ministry organized awareness activities with the Domestic Workers Union and the umbrella labor organization PIT/CNT.

Formal-sector companies generally complied with minimum wage regulations, and most workers earned more than the minimum wage. Many citizens and foreign workers were employed informally, however, and thus did not benefit from certain legal protections. By law workers may not be exposed to situations that endanger their health or safety and may remove themselves from such situations without jeopardy to their employment. Government authorities and unions protected employees who removed themselves from such activities. The Ministry of Agriculture is responsible for carrying out safety and health inspections in the agricultural sector.

The labor ministry reported 4,496 labor accidents in 2015, primarily in the construction and related services, agriculture and cattle breeding, health services and related activities, and manufacturing industries. The construction workers union reported eight deaths in 2015.